I0482980

This informational booklet is intended to provide a generic, non-exhaustive overview of a particular standards-related topic. This publication does not itself alter or determine compliance responsibilities, which are set forth in OSHA standards them-selves and the *Occupational Safety and Health Act*. Moreover, because interpretations and enforcement policy may change over time, for additional guidance on OSHA compliance require-ments, the reader should consult current and administrative inter-pretations and decisions by the Occupational Safety and Health Review Commission and the Courts.

This information will be made available to sensory impaired individuals upon request. Voice phone: (202) 693-2120;

The Occupational Health Professional's Services and Qualifications: Questions and Answers

U.S. Department of Labor

Occupational Safety and Health Administration

OSHA 3160

1999 (Revised)

Contents

Controlling occupational injuries and illnesses and related expenditures is a top priority in most companies. Selecting a qualified health care professional to participate in the workplace safety and health activities can be a vital step in this process. The following questions and answers are to provide guidance and serve as a resource for those considering such a selection.

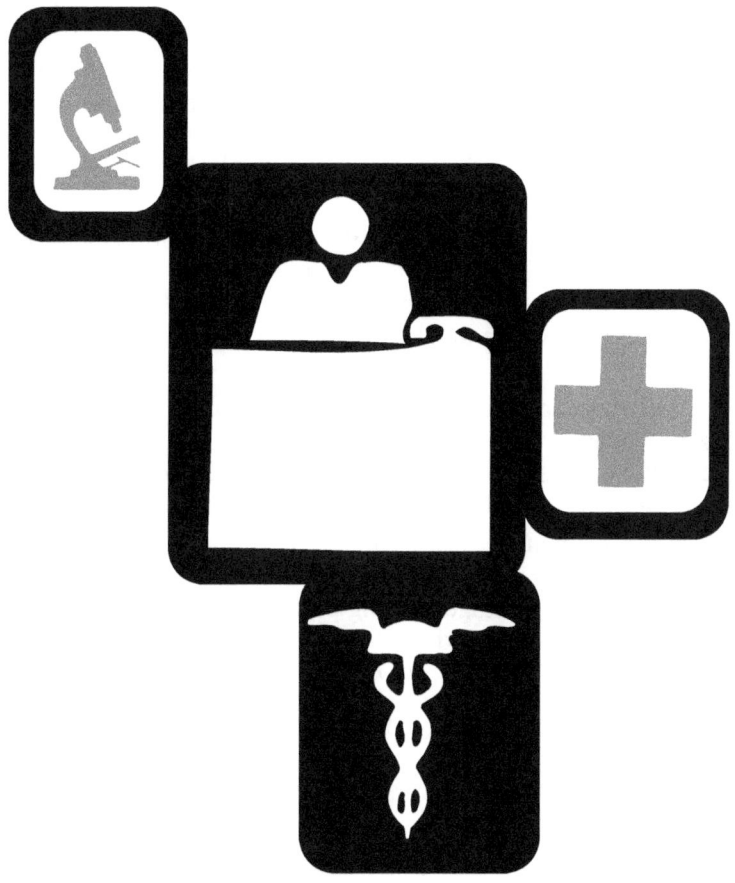

2 | What Issues Should be Considered in Selecting a Health Care Professional?

 A variety of health care professionals are available to employers. Selecting an appropriate provider for the worksite depends on a number of factors, including:

- The Occupational Safety and Health Administration's (OSHA) screening and surveillance requirements for specific substances or hazards associated with the worksite;
- The number, diversity, size, and seriousness of the hazards involved at the worksite(s); and
- The level of resources committed to an occupational health care service as part of a comprehensive safety and health program; and
- Distance to the closest trauma center or health care facility.

At a minimum, workplace safety and health involves management support, employee involvement, worksite analysis, hazard prevention and control, occupational health care management (including screening and surveillance for disease and injury), and training and education.

Qualified occupational health care professionals can assist the employer in achieving a safe and healthful work environment. Along with other safety and health professionals, health care professionals work collaboratively with labor and management to:

- Identify potential hazards and to find ways to prevent, eliminate, minimize, or reduce hazards;
- Develop and manage training programs to promote workplace health and safety; and
- Enhance the accuracy of OSHA recordkeeping.

What *Unique* Contributions Can an Occupational Health Care Professional Make to Workplace Safety and Health?

3

 Health care professionals are uniquely qualified to assess and treat illnesses and injuries. Health care professionals must have the appropriate licensure, registration, or certification. Additionally, they should have occupational health experience and expertise in management and be available on a full- or part-time basis, depending on the nature and size of worksite(s). They may be a permanent employee or hired on a contractual basis.

In addition to working collaboratively with other safety and health professionals, a qualified health care professional may be selected to:

- Provide screening related to specific chemicals or exposures, including preplacement (post-offer) physical examinations, job placement assessments, periodic examinations, and maintenance of confidential employee health records, including individual screening results.
- Manage and/or treat work-related illnesses and injuries, with emphasis on early recognition and intervention; make recommendations about work restrictions or removal; and follow up and monitor workers as they return to work.
- Develop and implement health promotion programs.
- Provide guidance for case management of employees who have prolonged or complex illnesses and injuries.

For small employers, or those with limited resources, one of several models for delivering occupational health care at the workplace can be considered. This might involve sharing the services of health care professionals within a business or industrial park, or contracting with a larger firm whose occupational health service includes an occupational health care professional as part of its total safety and health program. (See **References**: B. Burgel *Innovation at the Worksite.*)

Health care providers such as licensed practical nurses (LPNs) and emergency medical technicians/paramedics (EMTs) can augment the services of the physicians or registered nurse. Physician assistants (PAs) also contribute valuable services.

Whatever health care professional is chosen, the employer should ensure that the provider has expertise or experience in occupational health and safety as well as an understanding of occupational illnesses and injuries.

 Health care professionals qualified to design, manage, supervise, and deliver health care in occupational settings include a variety of practitioners. It is imperative, however, that the legal "scope of practice" unique to each state be considered prior to hiring or contracting for services. The "scope of practice" refers to the credentials, responsibilities, and legally authorized practice of health care professionals.

Physicians, physician assistants, and registered nurses, including nurse practitioners, receive standardized educations with core curricula (individualized to their profession) necessary to pass national or state boards and to be licensed in a particular state. Physicians and registered nurses are then eligible to become certified in a specialty practice, such as occupational medicine (physicians and physician assistants) or occupational health nursing (registered nurses and nurse practitioners), through a combination of additional specific education and experience. The additional educational training in occupational health typically includes course work in epidemiology, toxicology, industrial hygiene, recognition and management of occupational illnesses and injuries, research, and general management of a comprehensive occupational health program.

Physicians

Medical Doctors (MDs) have completed study at the college level and training at an accredited school. Licensed MDs have passed the National Medical Board Exam or equivalent examinations and have a license to practice within a given state(s).

Doctors of Osteopathy (DOs) graduate from college and an osteopathic school approved by the American Osteopathic Association. They must pass a state board examination to qualify for a license to practice within a given state(s).

Occupational Medicine Physicians are medical doctors or

doctors of osteopathy who have completed additional occupational medicine training or acquired on-site experience. Completion of additional residency training and further practice in occupational medicine enables physicians to pursue certification in occupational medicine after meeting rigorous qualifying standards and success-fully completing an examination in occupational medicine given by the American Board of Preventive Medicine (ABPM).

Registered Nurses

Registered Nurses (RNs) receive training and education at the college level and graduate from a state-approved school of nursing. They pass a state board examination and are granted a license to practice within a given state(s).

Nurse Practitioners (NPs) are registered nurses who are licensed in their state and have completed formal advanced education, usually at the master's level. NPs practice under their state *Nurse Practice Act*. Some NPs are certified in occupational health as a specialty area. NPs independently perform many health evaluation and care activities—including physical exams, common diagnostic and laboratory tests—and diagnose and treat employees who are ill or injured. They also can prescribe medications in most states. Addi-tionally, NPs work collaboratively with physicians.

Occupational Health Nurses (OHNs) are registered nurses and nurse practitioners with experience and additional education in occupational health. Certified occupational health nurses (COHN or COHN-S) obtain certification from the American Board for Occupa-tional Health Nurses after meeting rigorous qualifying educational and experience standards and successfully passing an occupational health nursing examination.

Physician Assistants

Physician Assistants (PAs) provide services with the supervision of a doctor of medicine or osteopathy. PAs may perform physical examinations, diagnose and treat illnesses, order and interpret tests, prescribe medications in most states, and plan and implement therapeutic interventions. PAs must graduate from an accredited physician assistant's program, pass a national certification exam, and be licensed by the state. Some PAs specialize in occupational medicine.

Other Health Care Providers

Other health care providers include licensed practical or vocational nurses and emergency medical technicians. Traditionally, these individuals are **not** licensed to practice independently. They have specific training and are usually certified or licensed by the educational institution where they received the training. Sometimes the state licenses or certifies these providers and usually the state's scope of practice outlines the specific work restrictions for these individuals. For example, usually these providers are required to work under the supervision of, or implement orders given by, licensed health care professionals such as MDs, DOs, RNs, PAs, and NPs, except when delivering first aid.

Licensed Practical/Vocational Nurses (LPN/LVNs) graduate from a program of practical nursing and must pass the state board examination. They are licensed by the state to perform certain specific health care activities, under the direct supervision of a physician or registered nurse.

Emergency Medical Technicians/Paramedics (EMTs) are prehospital providers trained to provide specific and limited emergency care. Some EMTs receive advanced training to become paramedics, which allows them to perform more advanced emergency procedures. EMTs are authorized to perform their duties by standing orders or protocols from physicians. They respond primarily to injuries and acute illnesses on a temporary basis and are **not** independently licensed to provide other medical care.

8

How Can an Employer Verify the Scope of Practice for Health Care Professionals in the Licensing State?

Each state has a unique legal description of the scope of practice for health care professionals. When it is necessary to verify a health care professional's scope of practice for the occupational setting, the individual state's licensing or certification board should be contacted, as follows:

Medical Doctor

State boards of medical examiners and professional licensure can provide information about an occupational physician's educational training and type of practice. The American Board of Medical Specialties (ABMS) publishes an annual list of certified occupational medicine specialists. The employer may refer to the ABMS listings in the reference department of most public libraries or call the Office of ABMS at (800) 776-2378.

Doctor of Osteopathy

Doctors of osteopathy are licensed by a board in each state. Listings may include Board of Medical Examiners, Licensing Examiners, Board of Osteopathic Examiners, Board of Medical Practice, or Medical Licensing Board of (name of particular state). The American Board of Medical Specialties (ABMS) publishes an annual list of certified occupational medicine specialists (see MD listing above).

Registered Nurse and Nurse Practitioner

The National Council of State Boards of Nursing [(312) 787-6555] has information on the regulation of nursing in each state. Generally, the American Nurses Association (ANA) [(202) 651-7000] certifies NPs. The American Board for Occupational Health Nurses (ABOHN) [(630) 789-5799] certifies RNs in the specialty of occupational health.

Physician Assistant

All states except Mississippi license physician assistants. PAs are licensed by the state medical board or by a separate licensing board. PAs are certified by the National Commission on Certification of Physician Assistants (NCCPA) [(770) 734-4500].

Emergency Medical Technician

The scope of practice for emergency medical technicians (EMTs) also varies from state to state. There are several practice levels of EMTs each determined by the number of hours of training and the range of procedures authorized. Each state has a director of EMTs listed in the telephone directory under State Government. The appropriate office may be contacted under the telephone directory subheading listed as either the Department of Health, Department of Public Health, or Department of Emergency Medical Services.

Licensed Vocational/Practical Nurse

The state board of nursing in each state is listed in the telephone directory and defines the scope of practice issues for licensed vocational or practical nurses LVNs/LPNs.

An occupational health care professional evaluates the interactions between employees' work and health in the workplace. To do this effectively, the occupational health care professional should possess the following skills and competencies:

- General knowledge of the work environment, including worksite operations; familiarity with the toxic properties of materials used by employees as well as the potential hazards and stressors of work processes and jobs or tasks.
- Ability to determine an employee's physical and emotional fitness for work.
- Ability to recognize, evaluate, treat, and/or refer occupational illnesses and injuries.
- Knowledge of workers' compensation laws; local, state, and federal regulatory requirements; and systems for maintaining health records.
- Ability to organize and manage the delivery of health care services.
- Knowledge of legal and ethical issues related to occupational health care practice.

In addition to administering the health care program and supervising health care personnel, the occupational health care professional should communicate with workers and managers at all levels. *Most importantly, the health care professional must maintain __confidentiality__ between the health care professional and the employee **as required by OSHA, professional ethics codes, and individual state privacy acts**. Management should only be provided the necessary information to make an informed and competent decision on occupational health and safety issues.*

Is There a Good Way to Evaluate the Qualifications of an Occupational Health Care Professional?

11

During the interview process, the following kinds of questions and issues are appropriate to evaluate prospective occupational health care professionals:

- What type of education/training does the candidate have?
    - Note graduation date and all degrees and type of specialty certification;
    - Titles of continuing education courses taken in the last 2 years;
    - Where and when licensed, registered, or certified (ask for documentation); and
    - Years of experience in occupational health.
- In what type of industries has the candidate had experience?
- What kind of management experience(s) has the candidate had? For how long?
- What does the candidate know about OSHA recordkeeping requirements?
- Has the candidate ever prepared for and/or participated in an OSHA inspection?
- Does the candidate know about workers' compensation laws in your state?
- Is the candidate familiar with the Americans with Disabilities Act?
- What kind of information does the candidate want to know about your business?
- How can the candidate develop or improve your safety and health program?

You should expect the candidate to ask you about the following:
- Facilities (type, location)
- Number of employees
- Work processes
- Known or potential hazards
- Application of standards and/or regulations
- Current method of providing occupational health care services
- Other health care providers involved in providing services
- Existence and specifics of a safety and health program
- Medical surveillance programs
- Collective bargaining contracts
- Previous OSHA citations

• References from current/previous employers or educational institutions should be requested.

What Is the Difference Between Occupational Health Care Professionals and Other Occupational Safety and Health Professionals?

13

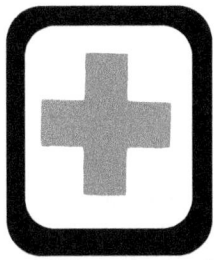 All occupational health and safety professionals are educated to have a proactive, preventive orientation, with the health and well-being of the employee as their primary focus. As mandated by each individual state, however, only health care professionals, within the scope of their practice, can assess and treat illness and injury beyond first aid. Additionally, health care professionals, based upon their education and training, can provide high-quality preventive health care information and programs.

The following descriptions highlight the overall skills and areas of competency of other occupational safety and health professionals who might be part of an effective safety and health program at your work site.

Industrial Hygienists

Industrial hygiene focuses on the identification and control of occupational health hazards arising as a result of or during work. The industrial hygienist focuses on the recognition, evaluation, and control of chemical, biological, or physical factors or stressors arising from the workplace, that may cause sickness, impaired health and well-being, or significant discomfort and inefficiency among workers or in the community. Professional industrial hygienists possess either a baccalaureate or master's degree in engineering, chemistry, biology, physics, or industrial hygiene.

The industrial hygienist monitors and uses analytical methods to detect the extent of occupational chemical, biological, or physical exposure and implements engineering controls and work practices to correct, reduce, or eliminate workplace hazards. Industrial hygienists can give expert opinion as to the magnitude of chemical, biological, or physical exposure, and the degree of associated risk. Certified industrial hygienists have passed a rigorous qualifying examination.

Industrial Engineers

Industrial engineering is the design, installation, and improvement of integrated systems of people, material, information, equipment, and energy. Industrial engineering draws upon specialized knowledge and skills in the mathematical, physical, and social sciences, together with principles and methods of engineering analysis and design to specify, predict, and evaluate the results obtained from such systems.

The Institute of Industrial Engineers has a special division devoted to ergonomics, and many industrial engineers elect to receive advanced training in this increasingly complex and growing specialty.

Safety Professionals

Safety professionals focus on developing procedures, standards, or systems to achieve the control or reduction of hazards and exposures that would be detrimental to people, property, and/or the environment. Certified safety professionals (CSPs) graduate from accredited college or university programs with a baccalaureate degree in safety and must have at least 4 years of professional safety experience prior to taking the Safety Fundamentals exam.

What OSHA Standards for General Industry Require Screening and Surveillance or Occupational Health Services?

15

The following OSHA General Industry Standards regulating toxic and hazardous substances have specific medical surveillance requirements in *Title 29 Code of Federal Regulations, Part 1910.*

Copies of OSHA regulations are available at cost from the Superintendent of Documents, U.S. Government Printing Office, Washington, DC 20402.

Please be advised that this list is subject to revision and expansion. It is the employer's responsibility to know the general and specific OSHA standards that apply to the industry and workplace.

General Industry Standards

2-Acetylaminofluorene	1910.1014
Acrylonitrile	1910.1045
alpha-Naphthylamine	1910.1004
4-Aminodiphenyl	1910.1011
Arsenic, Inorganic	1910.1018
Asbestos	1910.1001
Benzene	1910.1028
Benzidine	1910.1010
beta-Naphthylamine	1910.1009
beta-Propiolactone	1910.1013
bis-Chloromethyl Ether	1910.1008
Bloodborne Pathogens	1910.1030
1,3 Butadiene	1910.1051
Cadmium	1910.1027
Coke Ovens	1910.1029
Cotton Dust	1910.1043
1,2-dibromo-3-chloropropane	1910.1044
3,3' Dichlorobenzidiene (and its salts)	1910.1007
4-Dimethylaminoazobenzene	1910.1015
Ethylene Oxide	1910.1047
Ethyleneimine	1910.1012
Formaldehyde	1910.1048
Hazard Communication	1910.1200

Hazardous Waste and Emergency Response	1910.120
Lead	1910.1025
Methylene Chloride	1910.1052
Methyl Chloromethyl Ether	1910.1006
Methylenedianiline	1910.1050
4-Nitrobiphenyl	1910.1003
N-Nitrosodimethylamine	1910.1016
Occupational Exposure to Hazardous Chemicals in Laboratories	1910.1456
Respirators	1910.134
Vinyl Chloride	1910.1017

Some OSHA Standards that Require Occupational Health Services

Access to Employee Exposure and Medical Records	1910.1020
Confined Space	1910.146
Fire Protection	1910.156
Labor Camps	1910.142
Medical Services/First Aid	1910.151
Noise	1910.95
Pulpwood Logging	1910.266
Telecommunications	1910.268
Textiles	1910.262
Welding	1910.152

The following resources may be useful for additional information on occupational health care professionals in your area. The associations are typically the professional organizations for members of the profession. They work to increase awareness of the profession, as well as offer educational, service, and placement benefits for the members. Most have local, state, and/or regional chapters. Boards are generally the certification bodies for occupational health professionals and determine eligibility requirements. They also administer the certification exam and maintain directories of all certified professionals in a particular specialty. All telephone and fax numbers are accurate as of the date of printing; however, changes can be verified by local telephone directory assistance.

Medical Doctors

**American College of Occupational
and Environmental Medicine**
55 West Seegers Road
Arlington Heights, IL 60005
Phone (708) 228-6850
Fax (708) 228-1856
www.acoem.org

American Board of Preventive Medicine, Inc.
9950 West Lawrence Avenue, Suite 106
Schiller Park, IL 60176
Phone (847) 671-1750
Fax (847) 671-1751
www.abpremed.org

Osteopathic Doctors

American Osteopathic Association
142 E. Ontario Street
Chicago, IL 60611
Phone (312) 202-8000
Fax (312) 280-5893
www.aoa-net.org/affiliatedorg/state.htm

Occupational Health Nurses

American Association of Occupational Health Nurses
2920 Brandywine Road
Suite 100
Atlanta, GA 30341
Phone (770) 455-7757
Fax (770) 455-7271
www.aaohn.org

American Board for Occupational Health Nurses, Inc.
201 East Ogden Road
Suite 114
Hinsdale, IL 60521-3652
Phone (630) 789-5799
Fax (630) 789-8901
www.abohn.org

Nurse Practitioners

American Academy of Nurse Practitioners
P.O. Box 12846
Austin, TX 78711
Phone (512) 442-4262
Fax (512) 442-6469
www.aanp.org

Registered Nurses

American Nurses Association
600 Maryland Avenue, S.W., Suite 100
Washington, DC 20024
Phone (202) 651-7000
Fax (202) 651-7001
www.ana.org

Physician Assistants

American Academy of Physician Assistants
950 N. Washington Street
Alexandria, VA 22314-1552
Phone (703) 836-2272
Fax (703) 684-1924
www.aapa.org

**American Academy of Physician Assistants
  in Occupational Medicine**
950 N. Washington Street
Alexandria, VA 22314'
Phone (800) 596-4398
Fax (703) 684-1924
www.aapaom.org

Emergency Medical Technicians

National Registry of Emergency Medical Technicians
P.O. Box 29233
Columbus, OH 43229
Phone (614) 888-4484
Fax (614) 888-8920
www.nremt.org

National Association of Emergency Medical Technicians
408 Monroe Street
Clinton, MS 39056-4210
Phone (800) 34NAEMT
Phone (601) 924-7744
Fax (601) 924-7325
www.naemt.org

Industrial Hygienists

American Board of Industrial Hygiene
4600 W. Saginaw Street
Suite 101
Lansing, MI 48917
Phone (517) 321-2638
www.aiha.org

Safety Professionals

Board of Certified Safety Professionals of America
208 Burwash Avenue
Savory, Il 61874-9510
Phone (217) 359-9263
Fax (217) 359-0055

American Association of Occupational Health Nurses, Inc. (AAOHN). *Occupational Health Nursing: The Answer to Health Care Cost Containment.* Atlanta, GA: AAOHN. 1991.

American Academy of Nurse Practitioners (AANP). *Scope of Practice for Nurse Practitioners.* Austin, TX: AANP. 1993 (Revised).

American Academy of Physician Assistants (AAPA). *Physician Assistants: State Laws & Regulations.* 7th ed., Alexandria, VA:AAPA, 1998.

_____. "Various government and professional practice issue briefs." Alexandria, VA:AAPA, 1999. Online at http://www.aapa.org/.

American College of Occupational and Environmental Medicine. "Scope of Occupational and Environmental Health Programs and Practices," *Journal of Occupational Medicine* 34(4): 436-440, April 1992.

American College of Occupational and Environmental Medicine. "Code of Ethical Conduct," *Journal of Occupational Medicine* 36(1): 27-30, January, 1994.

Burgel, B. *Innovation at the Worksite.* American Nurses Publishing, 600 Maryland Avenue, S.W., Washington, DC 20024, 1993.

U.S. Department of Labor. Occupational Safety and Health Administration. *OSHA Handbook for Small Businesses (OSHA 2209).* Washington, DC: U.S. Government Printing Office, 1996 (Revised). Order Number 029-016-00176-0. $7.00

_____. "Safety and Health Program Management Guidelines; Issuance of Voluntary Guidelines Notice." *Federal Register* 54(16):3904-3916, January 26, 1989.

Single, free copies of the following and other publications can be obtained from OSHA field offices or the OSHA Publications Office, 200 Constitution Avenue, NW, Room N3101, Washington, DC 20210, (202) 693-1888, (202) 693-2498 (Fax).

All About OSHA - OSHA 2056

Access to Medical and Exposure Records - OSHA 3110

Asbestos Standards for General Industry - OSHA 3095

Chemical Hazard Communication - OSHA 3084

Consultation Services for the Employer - OSHA 3047

Employee Workplace Rights - OSHA 3021

Hearing Conservation - OSHA 3074

How to Prevent Needlestick Injuries: Answers to Some Important Questions - OSHA 3161

How to Prepare for Workplace Emergencies - OSHA 3088

Occupational Exposure to Bloodborne Pathogens - OSHA 3127

Occupational Exposure to Cadmium in the Construction Industry - OSHA 3139

Process Safety Management Guidelines for Compliance - OSHA 3133

Respiratory Protection - OSHA 3079

Working with Lead in the Construction Industry - OSHA 3142

The following publications are available from the Superintendent of Documents, U.S. Government Printing Office, Washington, DC 20402, (202) 512-1800. Include GPO Order No. and make checks payable to Superintendent of Documents.

OSHA Handbook for Small Businesses OSHA 2209 - Order Number 029-016-00176-0. $7.00.

Principal Emergency Response and Preparedness Requirements in OSHA Standards and Guidance for Safety and Health Programs OSHA 3122 - Order No. 029-016-00154-9; Cost $3.75.

Framework for a Comprehensive Health and Safety Program in the Hospital Environment - Order No.029-016-00149-2; Cost $3.50.

Code of Federal Regulations (CFR) Title 29 - General Industry 1901.1 to 1910.999 - Order No. 869-034-00104-1; Cost $44.00. 1910.1000 to End - Order No. 869-034-00105-0; Cost $27.00.

States administering their own occupational safety and health programs through plans approved under section 18(b) of the Occupational Safety and Health Act of 1970 must adopt standards and enforce requirements that are at least as effective as Federal requirements. There are currently 25 state plans: 23 cover private and public (State and local government) sectors and 2 cover the public sector only (Connecticut and New York).

COMMISSIONER
Alaska Department of Labor
1111 West 8th Street
P.O. Box 21149
Room 306
Juneau, AK 99802-1149
(907) 465-2700

DIRECTOR
Industrial Commissioner
of Arizona
800 W. Washington
Phoenix, AZ 85007
(602) 542-5795

DIRECTOR
California Department
of Industrial Relations
455 Golden Gate Avenue
10th Floor
San Francisco, CA 94102
(415) 703-5050

COMMISSIONER
Connecticut Department
of Labor
200 Folly Brooke Boulevard
Wethersfield, CT 06109
(860) 566-2211

DIRECTOR
Connecticut Department
of Labor
38 Wolcott Hill Road
Wethersfield, CT 06109
(860) 566-4550

DIRECTOR
Hawaii Department of Labor
   and Industrial Relations
830 Punchbowl Street
Honolulu, HI 96813
(808) 586-8844

COMMISSIONER
Indiana Department of Labor
State Office Building
402 West Washington Street
Room W195
Indianapolis, IN 46204
(317) 232-2378

COMMISSIONER
Iowa Division of Labor Services
1000 E. Grand Avenue
Des Moines, IA 50319
(515) 281-3447

SECRETARY
Kentucky Labor Cabinet
1047 U.S. Highway, 127 South,
Suite 2
Frankfort, KY 40601
(502) 564-3070

COMMISSIONER
Maryland Division of Labor
and Industry
Department of Licensing
and Regulation
1100 N. Eutaw Street
Room 613
Baltimore, MD 21201-2206
(410) 767-2215

DIRECTOR
Michigan Department
of Consumer
and Industry Services
4th Floor, Law Building
P.O. Box 30004
Lansing, MI 48909
(517) 373-7230

COMMISSIONER
Minnesota Department
of Labor and Industry
443 Lafayette Road
St. Paul, MN 55155
(612) 296-2342

ADMINISTRATOR
Nevada Division of Industrial
Relations
400 West King Street
Carson City, NV 89703
(702) 687-3032

SECRETARY
New Mexico Environment
Department
1190 St. Francis Drive
P.O. Box 26110
Santa Fe, NM 87502
(505) 827-2850

COMMISSIONER
New York Department of Labor
W. Averell Harriman State Office
Building - 12, Room 500
Albany, NY 12240
(518) 457-2741

COMMISSIONER
North Carolina Department
of Labor
4 West Edenton Street
Raleigh, NC 27601-1092
(919) 807-2900

ADMINISTRATOR
Oregon Department of Consumer
and Business Services
Occupational Safety and Health
Division (OR-OSHA)
350 Winter Street, NE
Room 430
Salem, OR 97310-0220
(503) 378-3272

SECRETARY
Puerto Rico Secretary
  of Labor and Human
  Resources
DOL and Human Resources
Prudencio Rivera Martinez
Building
505 Munoz Rivera Avenue
Hato Rey, PR 00918
(787) 754-2119

COMMISSIONER
South Carolina Department
  of Labor Licensing
  and Regulation
Koger Office Park
Kingstree Building
110 Centerview Drive
P.O. Box 11329
Columbia, SC 29210
(803) 896-4300

COMMISSIONER
Tennessee Department
  of Labor
710 James Robertson
  Parkway
Nashville, TN 37243-0659
(615) 741-2582

COMMISSIONER
Labor Commission of Utah
160 East 300 Street
3rd Floor
P.O. Box 146650
Salt Lake City, UT
  84114-6650
(801) 530-6901

COMMISSIONER
Vermont Department
  of Labor and Industry
National Life Building
Drawer 20
120 State Street
Montpelier, VT 05620-3401
(802) 828-2288

COMMISSIONER
Virginia Department of Labor
  and Industry
Powers-Taylor Building
13 South 13th Street
Richmond, VA 23219
(804) 786-2377

COMMISSIONER
Virgin Islands Department
  of Labor
2203 Church Street
Christiansted St. Croix,
  VI 00820-4660
(340) 773-1990

DIRECTOR
Washington Department
  of Labor and Industries
P.O. Box 44001
Olympia, WA 98504-4001
(360) 902-4200

ADMINISTRATOR
Worker's Safety and Compensa-
  tion Division (WSC)
Wyoming Department
  of Employment
Herschler Building, 2nd Floor
  East
122 West 25th Street
Cheyenne, WY 82002
(307) 777-7786

Consultation programs provide free services to employers who request help in identifying and correcting specific hazards, want to improve their safety and health programs, and/or need further assistance in training and education. Funded by OSHA and delivered by well-trained professional staff of state governments, consultation services are comprehensive, and include an appraisal of all workplace hazards, practices, and job safety and health programs; conferences and agreements with management; assistance in implementing recommendations; and a follow-up appraisal to ensure that any required corrections are made.

For more information on consultation programs, contact the appropriate office in your state listed below.

State	Telephone
Alabama	(205) 348-3033
Alaska	(907) 269-4957
Arizona	(602) 542-5795
Arkansas	(501) 682-4522
California	(415) 703-5270
Colorado	(970) 491-6151
Connecticut	(860) 566-4550
Delaware	(302) 761-8219
District of Columbia	(202) 576-6339
Florida	(850) 922-8955
Georgia	(404) 894-2643
Guam	011(671) 475-0136
Hawaii	(808) 586-9100
Idaho	(208) 426-3283
Illinois	(312) 814-2337
Indiana	(317) 232-2688
Iowa	(515) 965-7162
Kansas	(785) 296-7476
Kentucky	(502) 564-6895
Louisiana	(225) 342-9601
Maine	(207) 624-6460
Maryland	(410) 880-4970

Massachusetts ....(617) 727-3982
Michigan ....(517) 322-6823*(H)*
 ....(517) 322-1809*(S)*
Minnesota ....(612) 297-2393
Mississippi ....(601) 987-3981
Missouri ....(573) 751-3403
Montana ....(406) 444-6418
Nebraska ....(402) 471-4717
Nevada ....(702) 486-9140
New Hampshire ....(603) 271-2024
New Jersey...(609) 292-3923
New Mexico ....(505) 827-4230
New York ....(518) 457-2238
North Carolina ....(919) 807-2905
North Dakota ....(701) 328-5188
Ohio ....(614) 644-2246
Oklahoma ....(405) 528-1500
Oregon ....(503) 378-3272
Pennsylvania...(724) 357-2396
Puerto Rico ....(787) 754-2171
Rhode Island ....(401) 222-2438
South Carolina ....(803) 734-9614
South Dakota ....(605) 688-4101
Tennessee ....(615) 741-7036
Texas...(512) 440-3854
Utah ....(801) 530-6901
Vermont ....(802) 828-2765
Virginia...(804) 786-6359
Virgin Islands ....(809) 772-1315
Washington..(360) 902-5638
West Virginia...(304) 558-7890
Wisconsin ....(608) 266-8579*(H)*
 ....(414) 521-5063*(S)*
Wyoming ....(307) 777-7786

(H) - Health   (S) - Safety

Area	Telephone
Albany, NY	(518) 464-4338
Albuquerque, NM	(505) 248-5302
Allentown, PA	(610) 776-0592
Anchorage, AK	(907) 271-5152
Appleton, WI	(920) 734-4521
Austin, TX	(512) 916-5783
Avenel, NJ	(908) 750-3270
Bangor, ME	(207) 941-8177
Baton Rouge, LA	(225) 389-0474
Bayside, NY	(718) 279-9060
Bellevue, WA	(206) 553-7520
Billings, MT	(406) 247-7499
Birmingham, AL	(205) 731-1534
Bismarck, ND	(701) 250-4521
Boise, ID	(208) 321-2960
Bowmansville, NY	(716) 684-3891
Braintree, MA	(617) 565-6924
Bridgeport, CT	(203) 579-5581
Calumet City, IL	(708) 891-3800
Carson City, NV	(702) 885-6963
Charleston, WV	(304) 347-5937
Cincinnati, OH	(513) 841-4132
Cleveland, OH	(216) 522-3818
Columbia, SC	(803) 765-5904
Columbus, OH	(614) 469-5582
Concord, NH	(603) 225-1629
Corpus Christi, TX	(512) 888-3420
Dallas, TX	(214) 320-2400
Denver, CO	(303) 844-5285
Des Plaines, IL	(847) 803-4800
Des Moines, IA	(515) 284-4794
Englewood, CO	(303) 843-4515
Erie, PA	(814) 833-5758
Fort Lauderdale, FL	(954) 424-0242

Fort Worth, TX ....(817) 428-2470
Frankfort, KY ....(502) 227-7024
Harrisburg, PA ....(717) 782-3902
Hartford, CT ....(860) 240-3152
Hasbrouck Heights, NJ ....(201) 288-1700
Guaynabo, PR ....(787) 277-1560
Honolulu, HI ....(808) 541-2685
Houston, TX ....(281) 286-0583
Houston, TX ....(281) 591-2438
Indianapolis, IN ....(317) 226-7290
Jackson, MS..(601) 965-4606
Jacksonville, FL...(904) 232-2895
Kansas City, MO ....(816) 483-9531
Lansing, MI ....(517) 377-1892
Linthicum, MD ....(410) 865-2055
Little Rock, AR ....(501) 324-6291
Lubbock, TX..(806) 472-7681
Madison, WI ....(608) 264-5388
Marlton, NJ...(609) 757-5181
Methuen, MA ....(617) 565-8110
Milwaukee, WI...(414) 297-3315
Minneapolis, MN ....(612) 664-5460
Mobile, AL ....(334) 441-6131
Nashville, TN ....(615) 781-5423
New York, NY..(212) 466-2482
Norfolk, VA...(757) 441-3820
North Aurora, IL...(630) 896-8700
Oklahoma City, OK ....(405) 231-5351
Omaha, NE ....(402) 221-3182
Parsippany, NJ ....(973) 263-1003
Peoria, IL ....(309) 671-7033
Philadelphia, PA ....(215) 597-4955
Phoenix, AZ...(602) 640-2007
Pittsburgh, PA..(412) 395-4903
Portland, OR ....(503) 326-2251
Providence, RI ....(401) 528-4669

Raleigh, NC ....(919) 856-4770
Salt Lake City, UT ....(801) 487-0680
San Diego, CA ....(619) 557-2909
Savannah, GA ....(912) 652-4393
Smyrna, GA ....(770) 984-8700
Springfield, MA ....(413) 785-0123
St. Louis, MO ....(314) 425-4249
Syracuse, NY ....(315) 451-0808
Tampa, FL ....(813) 626-1177
Tarrytown, NY ....(914) 524-7510
Toledo, OH ....(419) 259-7542
Tucker, GA ....(770) 493-6644
Westbury, NY ....(516) 334-3344
Wichita, KS ....(316) 269-6644
Wilkes-Barre, PA ....(717) 826-6538
Wilmington, DE ....(302) 573-6115

U.S. Department of Labor
Occupational Safety and Health Administration
Regional Offices

Region I
(CT,* MA, ME, NH, RI, VT*)
JFK Federal Building
Room E-430
Boston, MA 02203
Telephone: (617) 565-9860

Region II
(NJ, NY,* PR,* VI*)
201 Varick Street
Room 670
New York, NY 10014
Telephone: (212) 337-2378

Region III
(DC, DE, MD,* PA, VA,*
WV)
Gateway Building, Suite 2100
3535 Market Street
Philadelphia, PA 19104
Telephone: (215) 596-1201

Region IV
(AL, FL, GA, KY,* MS, NC,*
SC,* TN*)
Atlanta Federal Center
61 Forsyth Street, SW,
Room 6T50
Atlanta, GA 30303
Telephone: (404) 562-2300

Region V
(IL, IN,* MI,* MN,* OH, WI)
230 South Dearborn Street
Room 3244
Chicago, IL 60604
Telephone: (312) 353-2220

Region VI
(AR, LA, NM,* OK, TX)
525 Griffin Street
Room 602
Dallas, TX 75202
Telephone: (214) 767-4731

Region VII
(IA,* KS, MO, NE)
City Center Square
1100 Main Street, Suite 800
Kansas City, MO 64105
Telephone: (816) 426-5861

Region VIII
(CO, MT, ND, SD, UT,* WY*)
1999 Broadway, Suite 1690
Denver, CO 80202-5716
Telephone: (303) 844-1600

Region IX
(American Samoa, AZ,* CA,*
Guam, HI,* NV,* Trust
Territories of the Pacific)
71 Stevenson Street
Room 420
San Francisco, CA 94105
Telephone: (415) 975-4310

Region X
(AK,* ID, OR,* WA*)
1111 Third Avenue
Suite 715
Seattle, WA 98101-3212
Telephone: (206) 553-5930

---

*These states and territories operate their own OSHA-approved job safety and health programs (Connecticut and New York plans cover public employees only). States with approved programs must have a standard that is identical to, or at least as effective as, the federal standard.